JOURNAL

PETER PAUPER PRESS, INC.
WHITE PLAINS, NEW YORK

Peter Pauper Press, Inc.
202 Mamaroneck Avenue
White Plains, NY 10601

ISBN 978-1-59359-666-8
Printed in China
7 6

Visit us at www.peterpauper.com